a Prayerbook *for* Volunteers

Deborah McCann

TWENTY-THIRD PUBLICATIONS
A Division of Bayard MYSTIC, CT 06355

Twenty-Third Publications
A Division of Bayard
185 Willow Street
P.O. Box 180
Mystic, CT 06355
(860) 536-2611
(800) 321-0411
www.twentythirdpublications.com

© Copyright 2001 Deborah McCann. All rights reserved.
No part of this publication may be reproduced in any manner
without prior written permission of the publisher.
Write to the Permissions Editor.

ISBN:1-58595-139-0
Printed in the U.S.A.

Contents

Introduction	1

ADVENT, CHRISTMAS, EPIPHANY	3
Keeping Peace	5
Make Us Instruments	6
The Giving Tree	7
Come, Thou Long Expected Savior	8
Christmas Morning	10
Mary	11
We Lift Our Voices...	12
Following Yonder Star	14
Same Old Same Old?	16

LENT, EASTER, AND BEYOND	
A Volunteer's Way of the Cross	20
Holy of Holies	35
Keep Our Hearts Burning	36
Pentecost—The Day of Days	37
Respite	38
Gearing Up	39
Back to Life!	40

THANKSGIVING	41

Christ has
No body on earth but yours;
No hands but yours;
No feet but yours;
Yours are the eyes
Through which he is to look out
Christ's compassion to the world;
Yours are the feet
With which he is to go about
Doing good;
Yours the hands
With which he is to bless now.

Teresa of Avila

Introduction

If you've ever volunteered for any task around your parish, you're probably no stranger to mixed feelings about the experience. On the one hand, you're delighted to be able to share your talents in a good cause. On the other hand, you may find that sharing becomes providing, sometimes exhaustively, and it can seem as if you're the only person in the parish ever called upon to do anything. (Beware of just standing around anywhere on the premises—an idle body is a body that can be put to work!)

Volunteers are the great unsung heroes of any endeavor. They are literally the glue that can hold an effort together and make it a success. Conversely, poorly trained volunteers, or those who don't find a happy match between their gifts and the expectations the parish may have, will be disillusioned and unwilling to serve again.

Jesus was surrounded by volunteers. And he still is today—all those amazing people helping out in our parishes, on our school playgrounds, teaching elective courses in the school or for the parish, running prayer groups and support groups for overworked parents and others. Not to mention those who turn their volunteer interest into service worthy of (though not always compensated as) professional commitment: liturgical ministers, religious education teachers, RCIA catechists, music ministers, choir members—the list goes on and on.

Volunteers come from all walks of life, and all have different personal reasons for wanting to serve. There are as many heartwarming and heartbreaking stories as there are individuals in our volunteer ranks. Volunteers deserve our support, our respect, and our prayers. I offer this prayerbook for all of them. As we travel through the seasons of the liturgical year, may the example of Christ on his journey to Calvary—and beyond—be a model for volunteers everywhere.

I dedicate this book to my husband Dan and my son Michael, who know this road all too well.

Advent
Christmas
Epiphany

Advent

These four weeks are so full of activity, I will understand completely if you don't find this section of the book until April at the earliest! Nonetheless, I would like to offer a few prayerful reflections on this busiest of seasons.

Whether you're chairing the parish Christmas bazaar (which probably means you've been up to your ears in red and green since August), directing/stage managing/providing music for the school Christmas play (and you may have to go out there a star if your lead actor doesn't show up), or running interference between the decoration committee and the liturgy committee (it could happen, even to a volunteer—remember, I warned you about standing around idle!), this can be a season of joy and anticipation.

"God surprises Earth with Heaven/Coming here on Christmas Day," goes the refrain of a song from the Iona community. In the midst of hectic, frantic busyness, there are still moments of grace. Don't worry, they'll wait for you to spot them.

Keeping Peace

God, grant me the serenity
    to smile cheerfully
    in acceptance and empathy
(and give me eyes to see and ears to hear).

God, grant me the courage
    to mediate if I can
    and to refuse if I can't
(and give me backbone to stand strong).

God, grant me the wisdom
    to be your witness and instrument
    so that this season will ring with peace
(and give me grace, so that I may speak
your name in blessing).

Make Us Instruments

Dear Lord,
we want to make a joyful noise for you.
We want to celebrate your immense gift to us
of your son.
We want to make the rafters ring with our jubilation.
Can you help us create beauty out of bedlam?
Can you once again form sense and shape
out of elements that clash and rupture?
Can you make that lion at least talk to that lamb,
and gift us with the sight to see
that even chaos sings your praises?
Be with us, Lord, as we raise our human voices
in your name,
ever and always,
our God, Emmanuel.
Amen.

The Giving Tree

Dear Lord,
my feet ache, my back aches,
my heart aches.
In this nation of plenty,
how can children be without warm mittens?
How can families be without so much?
Help me focus, Lord, on others.
Help me see them as my family,
As close in spirit as you are.
Help me make this Advent
a time of real sharing,
honest nurture,
and giving without measure.
Let me reflect your face
to all I meet.
Amen.

Come, Thou Long Expected Savior

Dear Lord,
once again this season has sped by,
leaving mayhem in its wake.
But the tree is up, the gifts are wrapped,
and the miracle is about to happen anew.
Thank you, Lord,
for the few moments in these weeks
when I saw your face,
heard your voice,
felt your touch.
This whole season I was surrounded
by clouds of witnesses.
Everyone I met was a reflection of you—
at least they were when I remembered they were.
Thank you, Lord,
for the few moments in these weeks
when I felt joyful anticipation
and could breathe the name "Emmanuel"
in wonder and awe.
Amen.

Christmas

When you go to church on Christmas, what do you see? Can you sit back and relax, enjoying the decorations, the warmth, the glorious music, the special touches that make this season so special?

Or do you see nothing but the flaws? Does each suspended garland represent hours of painstaking work? Do the figures in the manger remind you of your bad back or splinters? Are you so sick of the choral music you've been rehearsing that you're tempted to burst into "Lazy, Hazy, Crazy Days of Summer" instead of "Silent Night"? Do the shining altar vessels bring to mind endless polishing, when you would rather have been home taking care of your own holiday preparations?

If you're a dedicated volunteer, you probably experience a mixture of both satisfaction and frustration. There is perhaps no other season in the church year that calls for so much legwork on the part of volunteers.

Sometimes, frankly, you can be overwhelmed. There are just too many suitors for your limited time. But today, as the Christmas season ends for the outside world, let its spirit and promise begin to grow and take root in your heart. Carry the joy of our newborn savior with you throughout the next twelve days—the world is done with its celebrating; now it's time for your own special party.

Christmas Morning

Dear Lord,
please understand my reluctance
to join you in celebration today.
It's been a long Advent—
too few days, too few hours,
too much to get done.
The church looks beautiful,
a fitting and joyous place.
I just need time with my family.
I need time to thank my spouse
for all the hard work done on my behalf,
while I was serving here.
I need time to remember that my work was for you,
not for this building.
I need to be reminded of why you came,
which is why we serve,
which is why I am here after all.
Thank you, dear Lord, for surrounding me with love.
Thank you for the gift of yourself.
Thank you, after all is said and done,
for the chance to celebrate.
Tired and overwhelmed as I am,
in your presence my voice finds its song.
Amen.

Mary

Dear Lord,
thank you for the witness of your mother.
I find myself at loose ends just now,
weary with all the holiday chores,
barely able to remember what we're celebrating
(someone last night mentioned Easter preparations!).
But when I think of her,
young, afraid, carrying you within her,
I am humbled.
When I think of her,
heavy with child, wracked with pain,
birthing in a strange place,
I am humbled.
When I think of her,
full of joy, reflecting grace, and quietly proud,
I am humbled.
And I am grateful.
Thank you, Lord, for the witness of your mother.
Amen.

We Lift Our Voices

Dear Lord,
help me in my ministry
of sharing your message in song.
We sing of Christmas joy and wonder,
of a savior born and a world renewed.
We have sung these songs for months, Lord,
while the world rushed around us
in holiday madness,
and we felt left behind.
Help me remember, in these words
so often repeated,
that your message has been the same
for over two thousand years—
Peace. Joy in the morning. A redeemer born for us.
Let these words of light and life
infuse me and transform me
so that I may join my voice with these others
in heartfelt, unending praise of you.
Amen.

Epiphany

We have celebrated the twelve days of Christmas—I think. By now, the kids are back in school, we're back at work, and the decoration committee is getting ready to "strike the set" in church. But already, little by little, as the Magi have drawn closer to the Child, our thoughts have turned increasingly away from the mystery and miracle of the Incarnation. The world has entered in, and, if we did have a brief respite from all our responsibilities, it's over now.

Before we get involved with lenten and Easter planning (if it's not already done), let's try to take a moment to remember why we do what we do, and who we do it for.

Howard Thurman, a Baptist minister, reminds us that it is after the Magi have gone home, the star is gone, and the angels and shepherds have dispersed that the true work of Christmas begins—not only to feed the hungry, but to seek them out, to be Christ for others.

Let the feast of the Epiphany bring you to your own epiphany, and a new sense of purpose and commitment. Remember, the church couldn't survive without its volunteers—your role and presence are crucial. (And may I remember this as well!)

Following Yonder Star

Dear Lord,
now, as the wonder of your birth
is replaced by trees in the gutter,
help me to remember the glow of the star.
Now, as the majesty of angel song
is replaced by ringing phones and honking horns,
help me to remember the promise in their voices.
Now, as the miracle of God coming to be one with us
is replaced by routine and boredom,
help me to remember the glory of your amazing gift.
Most of all, dear Lord,
help me to share your good news
with everyone I meet.
Let this Epiphany fill me with new purpose
and vigor,
and change me into a bright and shining witness
of your love.
Amen.

Ordinary Time

The way our church year is set up, we have a few weeks of Ordinary Time between the Baptism of the Lord and the beginning of Lent. We don't get back to Ordinary Time until after Pentecost, when it goes on throughout the summer and fall, until the first Sunday of Advent rolls around again.

Those of us who volunteer can get a lot out of the Scriptures of this season. Depending on the year in the lectionary, you can hear such volunteer favorites as "Vanity of vanities! All is vanity!" or "...shake the dust from your feet in protest," or "Be doers of the word" or "Come to me, all who are weary...."

We hear a lot in this season about how to be good and effective disciples. And we hear a lot about serving others, and not counting the cost. In this day and age, that's an unlikely position to take. But Jesus asks us to be countercultural and to defy the status quo.

Volunteering won't make you famous, and it may not even get you liked, but if your main purpose in serving is to help God's kingdom come, and to work for God's greater glory, then you can have no higher purpose.

A wonderful holy woman I know once told me that people never asked her *if* she went to church. They always asked her *where* she went to church. If we keep to this life of service long enough, we too will begin to reflect a bit of God's glory!

Same Old Same Old?

Dear Lord,
whether we call this "Ordinary Time"
or "Sundays of the Year,"
it just doesn't have the punch or excitement
of the festal seasons.
Yes, that's right—
I, who spent so much time complaining about
how overworked and under-appreciated I was,
am now wishing for a little variety
in the sameness of my days.
Help me hear your word, Lord,
as you use these Sundays to mold me,
fashion me into a disciple.
Open my eyes to see those who are in need.
Open my ears to hear the cries of those
whose voices are seldom heard.
Open my heart to be your servant,
ever and always a witness to your mercy and love.
Help me use these Sundays to grow and flourish
in your sight.
Amen.

Lent Easter and Beyond

Lent

From Ash Wednesday to Holy Thursday, as winter finally loosens its grip and spring begins to show its face, we Catholics celebrate Lent.

The emphasis of this season is different for me now from the way it was when I was a child, with mite box in hand and a longing for the comic books I had promised not to read (or buy) all during the forty days. Now the idea of sacrifice is not just "giving something up," but giving up something of oneself to grow closer to God, removing barriers of pride or greed or selfishness that separate us, not from God's love (for that is infinite, unconditional, and always ours), but from our awareness of it, and our ultimate acceptance of its saving warmth.

During this season many volunteers will be working diligently with catechumens and candidates seeking full reception into the church at the Easter Vigil. These people who serve the church through the RCIA have an awesome task to fulfill—to present the faith by representing it. It's not enough to fill seekers' heads with doctrines and rules. It's the charge of anyone working with newcomers to acknowledge and respect where they are on their faith journey. That's a heady responsibility for a volunteer; no matter how many courses or workshops someone has taken, what it comes down to is compassion, understanding, and reaching out in love.

People seeking a welcome in our faith community have come to us from many different paths. Some have married into the faith, and have become more active parishioners than many of the "cradle Catholics" in the pews. Others have come because of a hunger they have not been able to satisfy, a search for meaning that has finally revealed itself in the words "God" and "Catholic." We need to make each person welcome, to show that it's okay to be countercultural in a world whose values are so different. We need to make everyone feel at home.

Lent can be a time of great discovery, for everyone in the parish. If you're sponsoring someone in the RCIA, congratulations! You'll learn as much if not more about the faith than the newcomers do. If you're in the choir, you'll be reminding us through your song and your silences that we are on holy ground. If you're on the decoration committee, you can use this time of sparseness in the church to uncover new ways of worshiping God in simplicity and dignity. If you're an usher, take the time to address parishioners by name. You'd be amazed how many people look to you as their one really human contact of the whole week. If you're "volunteering" just by showing up on Sundays, thank you! Without your presence nothing we do in church would have any meaning.

May Lent be a time of searching, questioning, renewing, and affirming our faith. Together we can grow so splendidly that our "Alleluia" on Easter morning will raise the roof.

For your lenten meditation, I would like to offer the following Way of the Cross for volunteers. Chances are you don't have much of a chance to make the Stations during the rest of the year, and you may be too busy to do them this year, too. But I hope you will see your own efforts mirrored in these reflections on the suffering and death of Jesus.

STATION ONE
Jesus Is Condemned to Death

"We need someone to run a couple of booths at the bazaar. They'll be next to each other, so it shouldn't be a problem, right?" "Say, listen, would you like to take up the collection today? One of the ushers is sick and we're shorthanded. And if you could hang around to help us count it after Mass, that'd be great. Thanks." "Hi! You're just the person I've been looking for. Help me unload the van...teach fourth-grade religion...be an RCIA sponsor...run the annual food drive...."

If any (or all) of this sounds familiar, you are a parish volunteer. Congratulations—though you probably feel sometimes a little like Jesus before Pilate. Everyone else has disappeared, and you are left on the scene, ready and able, but perhaps just a shade less than willing. You promise yourself next time it will be different. You'll be able to say no. But part of you doesn't want to say no. It's not that you feel that you're indispensable, it's that you look at each of these tasks as an opportunity to serve God and your parish a little more. It's just that sometimes, it's too much.

Jesus, help me to be discerning and wise in my choices for volunteering. Remind me of my true gifts, and let me praise you with them. Give me the courage to say no when my family needs me more. Thank you, Jesus. Let me serve you well.

STATION TWO
Jesus Takes Up His Cross

If you've said yes—yet again—you're now faced with a host of new challenges. You've got resentful people on all sides, those who think you're just trying to be important, your loved ones who won't be seeing very much of you for the duration of this task (even if you're stuffing envelopes at the kitchen table), and probably most of all, that inner voice telling you that this time you've taken on too much. It's not an unfamiliar voice. In fact, you hear it just about every time you agree to do something for the pastor/committee/altar society/director of religious education/prayer group. And any or all of these voices may be speaking important truths. Listen well, for God speaks to us through these voices. And God's ways are not ours.

Jesus, grant me the grace to work efficiently and well.
Help me to find the time to still praise you.
I don't want to lose sight of you or of those
who are important to me. Remind me this is only
temporary. Thank you, Jesus. Let me serve you well.

STATION THREE
Jesus Falls the First Time

How often in a volunteer situation do you feel totally responsible, as if the entire success or failure of the endeavor rests on your shoulders, and your shoulders alone? This is not an uncommon feeling, and if you're the kind of person who thinks the only way to get things done right is to do them yourself, you may be in for frustration at the very least, and self-hatred at the worst. It doesn't have to be that way. Ask people to help you. Jesus did no less—often. He picked people from the seashore, plucked them out of trees, took them from their jobs, and he delegated their tasks to them. More than that, he took time to pray, to discern where he was needed most and what was most important for him to do. Every major job can be broken into manageable components. Don't let yourself get overwhelmed. None of us has to function in a vacuum.

Jesus, help me to remain upright under the weight
of this task. Give me support at my right hand
and my left, and let me heed the advice
and suggestions of others on how to lighten the load.
Open my ears and my mind, and give me the grace
to hear and respond. Thank you, Jesus.
Let me serve you well.

STATION FOUR
Jesus Meets His Mother

Sooner or later, someone in our family, or one of our best friends, is bound to challenge us about the amount of time and effort we're expending for the parish. Listen well to these voices. Maybe you *are* spending too much time at church. Maybe you've forgotten how to just be with those you love. Are there issues at home that make parish work an escape, issues you really need to face? Is constant volunteering a way of avoiding a social life you might be wary of? Does the volume of your parish commitments increase as the tone of your family life goes flat? Can you make a promise now that as soon as this volunteer task is done you will face these issues openly and honestly? Or do you just really need a breather to get reacquainted with all the significant people in your life? Take that time—there will always be another volunteer task, but you only get one chance with your family. Where are you needed most?

Jesus, I need to know if I'm on the right path.
I have so many pressures from every side
that I've lost sight of my main purpose. I'm more
a burden than a help. Guide me and help me
to make good decisions. Thank you, Jesus.
Let me serve you well.

STATION FIVE
Jesus Receives Help from Simon

Simon of Cyrene—patron saint of volunteers. Pressed into service from the sidelines, he was chosen because he was there, he looked strong, and he didn't seem to be otherwise productively occupied. Sound familiar? There comes a time in every volunteer's life when the question arises: "How on earth did I get into this? What made me/them think I could do this? And where's the exit?" It's happened to us all—the offer to play guitar for the kindergarten picnic that turns into an invitation to take over the entire musical end of the Christmas pageant; the agreement to substitute for a sick playground volunteer that turns into a lifetime daily commitment—you know the drill. We can identify readily with Simon. Legend has it that Simon's sons became fervent disciples. So perhaps a bit of grace will rub off on whatever we are called to do. And maybe, just maybe, the added responsibilities are God's way of gently nudging us to greater and more fulfilling experiences as well.

Jesus, I want to help you in your work.
I want to be an asset to your church
and to be available and helpful to people who need
to see your face reflected in mine. Give me the grace
to accept opportunities gratefully and with confidence.
Let me feel your Spirit beside me.
Thank you, Jesus. Let me serve you well.

STATION SIX
Veronica Wipes Jesus' Face

It may not happen often, but when it does it's like a ray of sunshine cutting through storm clouds. We're up to our necks in duties, trying to eke out time and wherewithal to get things done when someone appears to help us. Maybe it's shouldering a great part of the burden, or just volunteering to run out for coffee and snacks for the crew. Maybe it's offering to make copies, or help out in your religion classroom. Maybe it's watching out for your kids after school or on a Saturday afternoon so that you can make that Christmas pageant rehearsal or decorate the hall for the spaghetti dinner. Whatever and whenever these hallowed moments come—snatch them! Seize them! Show your appreciation and gratitude, but never demur, never say everything's under control. Allow these people to help you. Being ministered to is the other half of being a minister. And you never know what new doors will open, what new lights you may cause to shine, when you let others in to share their gifts with you.

> *Jesus, I know that when I need help most desperately, that's when it will arrive, magically and miraculously at my side. Thank you for watching over me in these times, and thank you for knowing that I'm praying for help even when no words are forming. Keep me open to the invitations and offers of others.*
> *Thank you, Jesus. Let me serve you well.*

STATION SEVEN
Jesus Falls the Second Time

You're chairperson of the bazaar committee, and arrive at the major planning meeting to discover you're one of three people who showed up. You're the greeter and facilitator for the guest speaker for the adult education group, and you arrive to find that no refreshments are ready, no coffee is made, no chairs are set up—in short, nothing's been done. What happened to all the people who promised to help?! Once again you find yourself unfairly overworked and understaffed. Times like these can be all the justification the faithful volunteer needs to throw in the towel and vow never again to offer service in any capacity. Yet, somehow, if for no other definable reason than the greater glory of God, you manage to pull it all together, to get it up and running, and to do it well and in good humor. Later, when you collapse at home, you'll realize that your fatigue is a "good tired" that means that after all, there was enjoyment in the doing, and satisfaction in the result.

Jesus, help me to enjoy what I do in your service.
Keep my temper under control and my emotions
in check. Remind me that you are with me
at the lowest points as well as at the highest.
Thank you, Jesus. Let me serve you well.

STATION EIGHT
Jesus Admonishes the Women

I can think of no more glancing insult to give a volunteer than to say "I just don't know how you do it, time after time, and all by yourself! I ought to try running the bazaar myself sometime. You make it look so easy. How hard could it be?!" While you are still reeling from the blow, the "wellwisher" is gone, full of relief that once again credit has been given where credit was due—another crushing chore accomplished. Like the professional mourners who gathered around Jesus, you will always have your share of those who would not be caught dead volunteering themselves, but are thrilled that once again you've stepped into the breach. They're right up there with those who shake their heads and cluck over how tired you've been looking lately, and how you really should get some rest. These are the times when you just have to keep on smiling and praising God for the gift of a sense of humor. It may be your greatest saving grace!

Jesus, people are always patting me on the back
in relief that once again they didn't have to lift
a finger because I did. Keep me from crying
about how unfair it all is, and remind me
that next time I'll be different and not shoulder
everything myself. Thank you, Jesus.
Let me serve you well.

STATION NINE
Jesus Falls the Third Time

I've seen excellent, devoted, faithful people wrung to their very last smile, their very last kind word by parish leaders who have come to depend on them for just about everything. It's not that those who ask for volunteers are unfeeling or downright cruel, it's just that like the rich man who never saw Lazarus at his gate, they just don't see everything the volunteer is sacrificing to make whatever project it is turn out well. Perhaps the reason they don't see is because we don't tell them. We just grit our teeth in the "professional-no-problem" smile and soldier on. Those in charge need to hear how much *we* need us, instead of always telling us how much *they* need us. The door swings both ways, and we can set limits, boundaries, and priorities. Our fine organizational skills should at least occasionally be used for our own benefit.

> *Jesus, I want to be of service. I want to be*
> *an instrument of your peace. But it is all*
> *too demanding sometimes, and I don't think*
> *I can make it. I'm tired, and I'm angry,*
> *and I'm fed up. Keep me focused and grateful*
> *for your blessings. Thank you, Jesus.*
> *Let me serve you well.*

STATION TEN
Jesus Is Stripped

I have never understood the concept behind "You're so cute when you're mad." When I am angry (and, admittedly, close to madness), I am truly a sight. My son claims he has sometimes seen steam coming out of my ears. I wouldn't be surprised. If you've ever completely lost your temper and let 'er rip while serving in your volunteer capacity—or worse, blown up in front of the children you teach—you know how embarrassing and undignified such behavior can be (and it doesn't matter if it's not your fault!). Anger, righteous or not, can be a by-product of sacrificing time and talent. (Of course, if your motives for serving are clouded, then sacrifice itself can involve anger.) Ask yourself in those moments of exquisite self-pity and self-righteousness if perhaps you are more self-serving than being of service, more eager for praise than to be seen (or ignored) as the placidly humming wheel that makes everything go. Don't be too hard on yourself, though. This discontent is a decidedly human impulse. And God loves us in our humanity.

> *Jesus, help me to be your effective servant.*
> *Fill me with your light and love, and use me*
> *as a vibrant, joy-filled witness of your Way.*
> *Keep me peaceful, so I can bring peace.*
> *Thank you, Jesus. Let me serve you well.*

STATION ELEVEN
Jesus Is Crucified

There are times in any volunteer's life when, in spite of careful planning and all good intentions, the task falls flat. Nothing goes right. And there you are right in the center of the sightlines. Maybe it's a question of authority questioned or ignored, or the next person down the line dropped the ball, or maybe the whole project was a failure. Whatever the reason, this brings about the dark night of the soul, when the volunteer is sure to ask why. Don't be quick to assign blame, either to yourself or others. Try to cobble together a shred of common sense and objectivity, and let the situation go. There will be plenty of time to ruminate on it later. And who knows? Maybe this failure is a blessing in disguise. Either you'll analyze what went wrong and come up with a host of new and better ideas, or you won't ever be asked to volunteer for this (or any other!) task again. For a time, at least, would either outcome be so bad? God's ways are not our ways, and the Spirit moves through us, even when in spite of us.

> *Jesus, this project really failed. Help me to keep*
> *my head up high, and to try to serve you better*
> *next time around—in whatever way may*
> *bring you glory. Keep me safe in your embrace.*
> *Thank you, Jesus. Let me serve you well.*

STATION TWELVE
Jesus Dies

Alone, solitary, weary—there can be moments of fatigue and disgust and frustration that make all our efforts seem futile and without any kind of saving grace. We can become depressed and ready to chuck it all, and even our armor of humor has been pierced and punctured, leaving us empty and drained. No matter how much we've done, it isn't ever enough. We get done with one project and the next one is waiting right there for us— "Now that you're done reroofing the church and waterproofing the parish hall, won't you rewire the school and fill in for the DRE who's moving across the country?" It makes me tired just to write this! But if we can call on that glimmer of purpose that inspired our vocation to begin with, and be empowered by our ability to see what is possible for us rather than what people think we should do, perhaps we can begin to make better, more effective choices. The cross is only a symbol of starkness and failure for a little while—and only to us, who are seeing with our human eyes.

> *Jesus, thank you even for these dark times*
> *when my spirit is battered and nearly broken.*
> *Help me to remember the triumph your cross*
> *and death reveal. Refresh me and renew me.*
> *Thank you, Jesus. Let me serve you well.*

STATION THIRTEEN
Jesus Is Taken Down from the Cross

It was an acquaintance of Jesus who offered an unused tomb for his resting place. It was some of the less prominent disciples who attended to his remains. It's a humbling thought that the less important you think your contribution is, or the less valuable you think your role, the more fitting and right it is in the sight of God. The people who stick around to straighten the chairs and empty the coffee grounds, who make sure the lights are out and the doors locked, are just as important and valuable as the guest speakers or the committee heads who invited them. You may not feel you have any part to play, but nothing is insignificant when done cheerfully, with constancy and good will. Volunteering for the tiniest task lifts that task off someone else's shoulders. That is a gift, and known by others or not, it will be treasured.

Jesus, help me to remember that even the smallest task is great in your sight. Let even the simplest contribution I can make give you glory.
Thank you, Jesus. Let me serve you well.

STATION FOURTEEN
Jesus Is Placed in the Tomb

When all is said and done, there is a great satisfaction in contributing time and talent in the service of God and the church. You get to see the kids on the playground change and grow before your eyes. You know better than anyone how hard it is to get the candlesticks to shine like that. Someone new to the parish learned to read music and joined the choir because you took the time to take the ministry of welcome seriously. A child shyly thanks you and tells you you are the best teacher she ever had. We never know just how and where what we do is changing the lives of others for the better. Perhaps we're not making much of a difference in the people we may be trying to impress, or with whom we're having the biggest difficulties. But the couple in the second pew on the left is a little happier, the child on the jungle gym more confident, the classroom a warm and welcoming place, and we, if we are open to the depth of God's word and promise, are richer for the blessings poured back on us.

> *Jesus, thank you for the miracle of eyes to see*
> *and ears to hear your message in all the people*
> *we meet, all the jobs we undertake,*
> *and all the support and love we receive*
> *from our families. The strength of their love gives us*
> *courage to spread that love to others.*
> *Thank you, Jesus. Let me serve you well.*

Easter

I was an adult before I understood why Easter was a greater feast than Christmas. I had been away from the church for a number of years, but, true to form, when I returned it was with a zeal bordering on vengeance. I participated hungrily in my first Triduum, and was swept up in the solemnity and majesty of those holy three days. From the pageantry of Holy Thursday—the rituals of footwashing and the carrying of the Eucharist to its place of repose, followed by the silent stripping of the altar—to Good Friday's bareness and deep humility, to the Vigil's triumphant display of light conquering the darkness, as we read our salvation history from midnight until nearly three in the morning, I was hooked yet again on the faith of my birth.

Of course, nothing happens in a vacuum. I understand now that many people behind the scenes were at work creating the Great Liturgy we celebrated over those three days—many of them volunteers.

When we welcomed newcomers into our faith community that night, their faces were filled with a hope and trust that shone brighter than all the candles we had been holding before. They had found something in our midst—a warm handshake, a pleasant word, a sharing of experience (or maybe just a pew)—that spoke of who we are, who God is, and why we were eager to have them join us.

We are all volunteers when it comes to sharing of ourselves, and opening ourselves to the Christ revealed in others. Christ is risen! We are filled with joy!

Holy of Holies

Dear Lord,
we celebrated your rising when the sky was black.
We lit candles and sang songs
and heard our story.
Some of us handed those candles to those who entered,
some of us found places for the people to sit,
some of us practiced our readings
so that your word would reach hopeful hearts.
The church was packed last night;
it is packed this morning—
just like Christmas, your other holy holiday.
Some of these folks we see only for ashes, palms,
and Easter.
Some who come every day are displaced by the visitors.
Help me remember, Lord, to make everyone welcome.
This night could have been a chance for someone
to change, to grow, to come home to you.
Remind me that every face I see—angry, tired, bitter,
or sad—is a reflection of your face.
Help me to share your message
of joy and hope and unending love.
I stand as a witness, sinful yet saved.
Help me bring light to others.
Amen.

Keep Our Hearts Burning

Dear Lord,
after Easter Sunday, the real work begins.
The lilies need to be watered, pruned, replaced.
The fountain needs to be checked, and leaks mopped up.
The spilled candle wax needs to be removed.
Easter seems to be over,
the Great Three Days packed away again for another year.
Help me to remember that Easter Sunday is only
    the start,
the beginning of fifty days of wonder and awe and joy.
Like the weary, downcast disciples on the road
    to Emmaus,
I am let down by the end of the pageantry.
Next week, we'll be back to plenty of room.
Help me look for new faces, and make them welcome.
Help me remember to see you
in the breaking of the bread,
the sharing of the cup,
and the faces of your children.
Help me to know you as I serve you,
and to make your church a home.
Amen.

Pentecost — The Day of Days

Dear Lord,
thank you for this day of days.
This is the feast I remember
at those times when I feel full of your grace,
when serving others is a joy,
when things fall into place, and everything gets done.
This is the feast I remember
at those times when I feel lost and alone,
when serving others is a chore at best,
when things fall apart, and nothing turns out right.
A feast for all seasons, yes!
For your Spirit is with me, guiding me through.
Whether good or bad,
the days are suffused with your power—
when I remember to step aside and let you shine.
Sometimes I am so filled with wonder
I cannot speak.
Sometimes I am so filled with anger
I should not speak.
In either case, I am your vessel, your tool.
Use me well.
Dirty me up with frequent use.
Thank you for this day of days
when I remember who I am—and why.
Amen.

Respite

Dear Lord,
the lazy days are here.
I thought I would feel set adrift
in this season of slowness and inactivity around here.
Instead, I enjoy the time.
For once I have a chance to recharge the batteries,
enjoy my loved ones,
and seek you where you would be found.
I see you in church more than ever
(fewer faces make the sight of you even more precious).
I see you in the city and the country.
I see you in my children.
I see you in my spouse.
I see you in my friends.
I glory in the warmth of the sun;
even when the heat is oppressive,
it reminds me of your all-consuming love.
I enjoy this time
of remembering you,
and look forward (really!)
to serving you more.
Amen.

Gearing Up

Dear Lord,
it's August, and the calendar is filling up.
The choir is looking toward Advent,
the school is filled with teachers readying their rooms,
committees and parish groups are setting their schedules,
and the church is a little more expectant,
waiting for the return of summer travelers.
While I'm sorry to leave the contemplative days behind,
they have led me to new purpose.
I think I'm ready to start again.
I hope I'm ready to start again.
Give me clear eyes and a keen spirit, Lord,
to do your will with a happy heart.
Keep me free from pettiness, gossip, and showing off.
Remind me that it is you who are to shine—
through me, not in spite of me.
Help me keep my sense of humor,
so that in the rough times,
we can laugh together
at the foibles of the glorious humanity
you have created.
Amen.

Back to Life!

Dear Lord,
the days are turning crisp, and darker in the morning.
The kids are back in school, and my days should be freer.
But it's amazing how little time I seem to have.
Working to help build the kingdom eats up the time!
There are always people to help,
things to do,
meetings to attend,
events to plan.
Help me to seize each task with enthusiasm,
to do my best in all that I do for you.
I need your help for this, Lord,
I cannot do it alone.
Thank you for your guidance,
your Spirit,
and your constant love and light.
They spur me on,
they give me hope.
May your kingdom come—
with a little help from your friends!
Amen.

Thanksgiving

We have come to the end of the church year. Advent is almost always right on the heels of Thanksgiving. How wonderful and appropriate that is, to have a chance to gather and thank God for all God's goodness—right before we barrel back into the maelstrom, with a whole new year of service, headaches, heartaches, and unbelievable joys ahead.

I hope these reflections and meditations have touched some familiar chords in you. It has been my great pleasure and privilege to try and celebrate volunteers everywhere—often unsung and under-appreciated, but crucial and indispensable to any endeavor.

Know that you are valued, esteemed, and loved—and that the church and the world would be a poorer place without your shining witness!

With God all things are possible—with volunteers, all things get done!

My God,
I am Yours
for time and eternity.
Teach me to cast myself entirely
into the arms of
Your loving Providence
with the most lively, unlimited
confidence in Your
compassionate, tender pity.
Grant me,
O most merciful Redeemer,
that whatever
You ordain or permit
may be acceptable to me.
Take from my heart all painful anxiety;
suffer nothing to sadden me but sin,
nothing to delight me but the hope
of coming to the possession of You,
my God and my all,
in your everlasting Kingdom. Amen.

Catherine McAuley

Of Related Interest...

A Prayerbook for Catechists
Gwen Costello

Drawing on her own experience as catechist and DRE, this popular author offers prayers from the heart for a variety of seasons and situations. Each prayer reflects a firm belief in God's loving care for catechists and students, in the uniqueness of each child, and in the importance of the catechist's vocation. 0-89622-979-3, 48 pp, $5.95 (J-26)

A Teacher's Prayerbook
To Know and Love Your Students
Ginger Farry

Prayer poems for and about students are followed by brief reflections or questions for teachers to ponder in relation to their own students; others chronicle the good and bad days, the joys and disappointments in the life of a teacher. 0-89622-727-8, 64 pp, $4.95 (M-89)

A Prayerbook for Catechumens
Alison Berger

This book will help catechumens, directors, and RCIA teams unlock the riches of both the RCIA process and Catholic prayer tradition. The prayer experiences are organized into three main sections: the liturgy and the word of God; the rites and rituals of the RCIA process; and personal prayer. Simple to use and rich in context. 1-58595-147-1, 112 pp, $9.95 (J-92)

A Single Mother's Prayerbook
Ginger Farry

Here are the prayers of a single mom who called upon God in child-rearing situations as well as in times of loneliness and frustration. Through them the reader learns that we are never alone and that God is always present.

0-89622-973-4, 64 pp, $7.95 (J-17)

Available at religious bookstores or from:

TWENTY-THIRD PUBLICATIONS
A Division of Bayard PO BOX 180 • MYSTIC, CT 06355
1-800-321-0411 • FAX: 1-800-572-0788 • E-MAIL: ttpubs@aol.com
www.twentythirdpublications.com

Call for a free catalog